BY *Actors,*
FOR *Actors*

Excalibur Publishing
New York

© 1993 Excalibur Publishing

Published by:
Excalibur Publishing
434 Avenue of the Americas, Suite 790
New York, NY 10011

Cover design: Peter J. Byrnes

Library of Congress Cataloging in Publication Data

Gaffigan, Catherine.
    By actors, for actors.

    1. Acting. 2. Monologues. 3. Drama--Collections.
I. Title.
PN2080.G34   1991   812'.04508   91-74160
ISBN 0-9627226-5-0 (pbk.)

Printed in the United States of America

Table of Contents

MONOLOGUES

Female

Male

PERFORMANCE PIECES

Female

Male

SCENES

Male/Female

INTRODUCTION

By Actors, For Actors was originally conceived as a single book. But thanks to an immense response from writers and performers, *By Actors, For Actors* is now a series — with no end in sight.

If you are just beginning your career, or if you have no substantial training in the selection and presentation of monologues, please refer to the Introduction in Volume 1. There you will find valuable information about how to select a monologue which is particularly suitable for you, along with step-by-step instructions for preparation and presentation.

In line with the original concept of *By Actors, For Actos*, this volume contains original — and therefore unique — monologues of great diversity. You will find here monologues for women and men of all ages, from serious to serio-comic to comic. In addition, there are two original two-character scenes, which are useful class exercises.

With this volume, we are also introducing **Performance Pieces**. These are long monologues — too long for auditions — that are useful for solo performers or classroom work. (For permission to use any of the material in this book for public performance, contact the publisher.)

Acknowledgments

We are deeply indebted to each contributing writer whose work appears here, and I personally thank each one of them. The writer's gift of intense personal experience so generously shared is a gift to us all.

Once again, my special thanks to Sharon Good — I enjoy being on the team with her!

An Invitation

Most of the monologues in this volume were written by actors and actresses, based on real-life events. We invite you to tell us your story for publication in future volumes of *By Actors, For Actors*. All types of material are welcome. If you are concerned about your writing style, just write in stream of consciousness. Or just dictate the material onto a cassette and send that along. Editing will shape and focus the material for the performers to use. Selections from unpublished plays may also be submitted.

Send all submissions to: Excalibur Publishing, 434 Avenue of the Americas, Suite 790, New York, NY 10011, Attn: *By Actors, For Actors*. Please be sure to include your name, address including zip code, telephone number(s) and social security number. Include a stamped, self-addressed envelope if you want the material returned to you. For a copy of Submission Guidelines and compensation information, send a stamped, self-addressed envelope to the same address.

We welcome your remembrances, your joys, loves, sorrows, your life's events — this is the drama needed for monologues that are gripping and unique.

Please note that in addition to future volumes of *By Actors, For Actors*, we're also planning a special volume devoted to young people. (Send submissions to the address above, Attn: *By Kids, For Kids.*) So get those kids and teens writing, too!

Catherine Gaffigan
New York City, 1993

Monologues

Candy
from *Street Kid*
by David Mead

Okay! You win. My name is Parsons, Janie Parsons. I come from Boulder, Colorado. I've been in town for about a year. On the street about eleven months. Both my parents are dead, and there are no relatives. None that wants me. I'm 17. Really, I am!

What about Shadow? I didn't meet Shadow. You don't meet Shadow. He meets you. Usually in the bus station. At least, that's where I met . . . he met me. I was having breakfast at the McDonald's, and he sat down next to me. We got to talking. He asked if I knew anybody. I didn't, so he offered to put me up for the night. Dumb, huh? Well, maybe not so much. I was down to my last five bucks. I needed a place to hang out. And he was sharp-looking. You know, not handsome or a hunk or anything, but sharp. And he talked that rappin' street talk, and I thought he was pretty cool. So I went with him. And then I stayed with him for a month. And he was nice. I mean it, real nice! He didn't hit me or anything, and he made me feel good. Then about a month after I'd been there, his place, he told me I had to leave. It wasn't nasty or anything. He was real sorry to make me go, but he said he couldn't afford to keep me any longer. Something about his payments getting higher, or his rent going up. Some shit like that. So I said I'd go to work, help pay for my keep. But I couldn't do nothing. I didn't know how. I tried to get work, but nobody would hire me. I was underage. I did try, though. For two solid weeks I tried. Then I came home one night. I think it was the first week in January. I was all frustrated and pissed off, because I couldn't get work. And Shadow was there . . . with a friend. A big, good-looking guy. Shadow called him Punch. And he was a hunk. I mean, my jaw just hit the floor looking at him. Anyway, we got to talking, and he said he liked my looks. Like "sugar candy" ready to lick. By that time, I was getting the picture. I thought about getting mad. About slugging Shadow. But something stopped me. It wasn't fear. I wasn't afraid of Shadow. I was a little of Punch, but not Shadow. He was a 100 pound weakling.

But I was thinking about where I would go and what I could do. I got up and went into the next room. I started packing. Shadow came in after me. He tried to talk me into staying. I told him to go fuck himself. He told me I'd starve. That I wouldn't last ten days, unless I started working the streets. And if I did that on my own, I'd get ripped off or sliced up or maybe killed. I threw something at him. I don't remember what. Then I started to cry.

That night I slept with Punch. And I slept with Punch once a week for the next couple of months. By then, I was full time on the street. You're thinking it, aren't you? Another stupid, little cunt. A dumb country bitch gets took by some quick-talking nigger pimp. But I wouldn't be here if it wasn't for guys like you. You and all those other do-gooders out there. People who have ideas about how everybody else should live and act and dress. You're the bastards who ought to be locked up. Shadow's only trying to make a living. And he protects me. He runs off guys that look psycho, and he pays off the beat cop. And he got me out of Juvenile twice, put up the bail and everything. He doesn't take too much of my earnings either. A fair price for the work he does. And where was I going to go anyway?

I hate the street. But it's better than Boulder. You know what a virgin is in Boulder, Colorado? Any girl who can run faster than her stepfather.

Homework
by Leslie Reed

I was in the kitchen doing my homework. Everything around me was white. All the appliances were shiny, even in the shadows. The only light was above the table, where I was sitting with my school books in front of me. I was writing in my notebook. I could see through the sliding glass doors that it was dark out. The clock said eight o'clock.

My Dad was there, pacing back and forth past the refrigerator. He looked infuriated. He opened the refrigerator and took out a bottle of soda and poured himself a glass. His nostrils were flaring, his eyes red and bulging. He was mumbling. There was a lump on his forehead, and it seemed to be getting bigger the angrier he got. He looked at me and said in a very loud and angry voice, "Where is that bitch? She was supposed to be home hours ago." I felt myself crumple into a little ball, and I could hear myself saying, "I don't know." He kept pacing, and I tried to go back to my books, but he yelled again, and I jumped back to attention. "I don't believe that woman," he yelled. "She said she was going to drop something off at Mrs. Coppola's, and that was three hours ago. That fucking bitch, she must have gone shopping or something. Where the hell is she, God damned fucking bitch?"

He kept screaming and looked at me as if I were her. I felt impotent and afraid. I wanted to get away from the table, but I felt trapped. I was frozen. He gulped the soda down and opened the refrigerator again. He grabbed some cold cuts and stuffed them into his mouth, chewing with his mouth open like an animal at the kill. Then he slammed the refrigerator shut and came toward me, still chewing. I thought he was going to kill me. But he went right past me and pulled the sliding door open with such force that the door shattered all over him and all over the floor. Still yelling about "that bitch," he raced out of the kitchen and went upstairs to his room. I just sat there in the dim light and looked at the thousand tiny bits of glass that were all over the floor.

Finding Myself in the Holy Land
by Sharon Good

Have you ever been to Israel? It's a pretty incredible place. Wait a minute. Let me qualify this. I'm Jewish, but I'm not religious. More anti-religious, if anything. The only reason I went to Israel is because my sister was living there, and my parents and I went to visit her. Believe me, it was no pilgrimage or religious quest. I was curious, though. Think of it. In this country, when you see something old, it's maybe three or four hundred years at most. But in Israel . . . well, we stood on the hills of Jericho where Joshua stood. We walked where Christ walked. We stood where he gave the Sermon on the Mount, and we looked down the hill to the Sea of Galilee, just like he did. Pretty incredible stuff. Right out of the Bible, which, by the way, the Israelis read like a history book.

Anyway, something happened to me when I was there. My sister took us to this museum, the Museum of the Diaspora, in Tel Aviv. It's a great museum. They have all these multimedia exhibits about the Jewish people from the time they were scattered from the Holy Land thousands of years ago. I really got into it, totally absorbed by these displays. As I went through the museum, for the first time in my life, I began to feel a part of something. I felt that these were my people, and I was proud of it. I saw that being Jewish is much more than being claimed by a religion. It's a people, a culture, a foundation . . . my foundation. Suddenly, this part of me that had been empty for as long as I can remember filled, and I felt whole again. My eyes clouded over. I saw people looking at me, so I ducked into a stairwell and stood there for a few minutes, savoring the feeling. When I felt capable of speaking again, I went back in and found my family. I looked at my parents, and something seemed different about them. They were no longer the people who nagged me to do my homework and stand up straight, but the first link in a chain that stretched from me all the way back to Moses. I started to cry again and hugged them. "What's this?" they wanted to know. "I just love you." My Dad shook his head and chuckled, and my Mom shrugged her shoulders, and we continued through the museum.

And no, I didn't decide to move to Israel and live on a kibbutz. What I found was inside of me, and it didn't depend on geography. And no, it didn't deter me from a life of crime or anything dramatic like that. All that happened was a small miracle. I found out who I am. That's all. And as they say, it's the small miracles that really matter.

Memo to Freud from a player
by Signe Hasso

Human nature is,
to say the least,
an extraordinary thing.
How human it is
depends on the beast
roaringly hovering within
your body and soul,
aiming to capture them both,
leaving nothing at all.

Born to this tangible Earth
and stunned by the birth,
if happy or sad,
you're faced with the task
of forever keep coping,
forever keep sorting
what's said to be good
from what's said to be bad —
allow joy its full reign,
even if not understood
and thought of as mad.

So it goes.
As no one really knows
who's who or what's what,
why bother to ask?
Trying to live as you please
is being sufficiently human
if done with some grace
and pliable ease.
If others think not,
so what —let them be.
Blame the beast who, bewildered,
no longer roaring with glee,

is still hovering within
what's left of body and soul
and hating it all.

It's clear as can be —
whatever you think,
what you've learned
and really know
is, most of the time,
to both friend and foe,
not at all so.
Are they wrong?
Maybe right?
Who the hell knows,
so why fight.

Yet, trying to stay
what's considered as sane
may not be in vain.
Even if odds are at odds
and it seems a bit late,
one thing is left —
a game — not branded sin
or called theft.
You gamble on fate
and you gamble big,
placing your bets
not only to show or place
to merely save face.
You gamble all that you have,
including the beast.
You gamble with poise
and with flair.
It's hope in the air.
There always is
when gambling on fate
and betting to win.

A Forgotten Treasure
by Annie M. Taylor

It was raining outside, one of those days when you don't mind being indoors. What better thing to do than throw out some of those things you save because of wonderful memories. I opened a drawer, which had not been open for years, and pulled out a piece of terry cloth, which had a pocket attached. I remembered it was from a robe I really treasured. I had searched far and wide for the right robe. It was aquamarine. I could use it as a beach robe, a shower robe, or just to sit around the house as a fancy housecoat. It had served me well for the first week of my vacation. As I turned this piece over in my hand, I noticed a couple of dark brown spots on it, and it brought back to mind why I had it and why this was all I had left.

When my Canadian pen pal — we'd been writing for seven years — told me he was going to Turkey for a month's vacation with a Turkish friend, I asked if they were going to take me. I was as surprised as my family and friends, when they received postcards from me from Greece and Turkey.

Now, twenty years later, I was holding in my hand a piece of material from that big event. Once again, I looked at those brown spots and remembered. We had hired a private cab in Manisa, where our Turkish friend was born and his family still lived. We would use it to tour around the country. After touring Izmir, Alanya, Pamukkale, and many other places of interest, we decided to return to Istanbul. We did all of our driving during the day. I did not know that Turkey is a very mountainous country. At the time I was there, they didn't have the best of roads. I will not mention their driving.

As we were climbing up a mountainside, we were on

the right hand side of the road, against the mountain. I suddenly saw what, at the time, appeared to be a toy bus fly across the front of our car. Of course, the next minute, I realized it wasn't a toy, but a real bus, loaded with people, that had gone over the cliff. We stopped the car to get out. My companions insisted I stay in the car. But when I saw people climbing up the embankment with their injuries, blood everywhere, I opened up my suitcase to see if I had anything for bandages. The only thing of any use was my robe, some talcum powder and some witch hazel. Without a second thought, I tore up the robe into strips and bandaged up as many as I could. Soon the police and other help arrived, and we were on our way. It was then that I passed out.

There is another piece of terry cloth of green and white. When we arrived at my Turkish friend's home in Izmir, he told his family about my using my bathrobe for bandages. His mother and sister spent the next evening hand sewing me another robe from material that my companions had purchased. I wore that robe until it was threadbare.

I have many wonderful memories from my trip to Turkey, but that little remnant from a robe made just for me is very, very special.

Home for Thanksgiving
by Peggy Peters

We looked forward to Thanksgiving, when our sons John and Paul would be home from school for the holiday weekend. John arrived home on Wednesday with two friends from his fraternity house in Seattle. We had a lovely family Thanksgiving, all together. The next evening, John picked up his friend David, and they met their other fraternity brothers downtown. Later that evening, he took David back home, they chatted awhile, then John drove off — and eight houses later came to an intersection, where he was hit broadside by a pick-up truck, and our John was killed.

The paramedics revived him with CPR, and he was taken to Sacred Heart Hospital. He was bleeding internally, and they replaced four pints of blood. John was attended by a neurosurgeon and a vascular surgeon, and they examined and x-rayed him to find out why he was bleeding and in a deep coma. His body wasn't hurt anywhere that we could see. We waited four long, agonizing hours, praying that God would spare him. They finally discovered that John had a transection of the spinal cord. That means a separation of the base of his skull from the first vertebra. There was nothing that could be done for him, as he lay on the trauma board on the life support.

The surgeons came to talk to us after each test. Finally, the neurosurgeon came in for the last time, and I knew exactly what he was going to ask. I told him that, since he could not help John, he had better give him to God. We were finally allowed to see our dying son, and I kissed his face and curly-haired head and told him how much we loved him. He was still on the life support system, because they asked if we would wish to donate his kidneys and eyes.

It is a heart-breaking experience, which we will live with all our days. Our John was suddenly torn from our lives and family. Dreams of his graduation, his career, his own children, all shattered. True, it happens every day — with other families — through sickness, accident, but it is so very hard to understand, and in spite of our faith, I ask God, "Why?"

Time, as always, is a great healer of a broken heart, but the pain never really goes away. We are fortunate to have other children. But it makes one wonder why a child is sent, to watch him grow up into a strong, athletic young man, who matures and becomes responsible, wanting an education. Then, one early winter morning, he's gone, and so are the dreams. It is all a great mystery, and now our hope is that if it be His will, we'll rejoin our son and spend eternity together. John's death has had a great effect on our family, and we have been drawn closer. We call one another more often, write more often, because we have learned that life is very fragile. No one has a special lease on life. No one is exempt.

On the Bamboo
by Francine M. Storey

I saw them. I saw The Grand Kabuki! What a transcendent experience! Now, the plot was a bit complicated. The star wasn't really a man, but a fox who was looking for his parents, but the lady didn't know that. There's a lot of things women don't know about men. There's a lot of disguise in the kabuki. Men who are foxes, men who are women who are monsters, warriors who are evil priests, and everyone has his face painted white. But anyway, not to worry, everything ended happily with a troupe of acrobats standing on each others' shoulders.

Now came an interlude to allow the musicians to perform alone. The koto player began to strum a lamentful sound, and the singer began to, well, sort of gargle. It was this morbid combination of moans and grunts and shouts all rolled up into one. Ahooo . . . ah . . . wah . . . uggh . . . wooo. It wasn't a song at all, but a sound that didn't belong to the world as I knew it.

And I couldn't help it — I tried not to, I really did — but I began to think about World War II. Guadalcanal, Iwo Jima, the March of Bataan, Burma, the prison camps, the Japanese spearing British soldiers for bayonet practice. Don't get me wrong. That war is all over, and I know it. We've totally forgiven each other. America has forgiven Japan for Pearl Harbor, and Japan has forgiven America for Hiroshima and Nagasaki. It was a terrible mistake on everyone's part. We're all bad. All countries do bad things, and most people are potentially awful.

But I tried, I really tried, but I couldn't stop thinking about this incident that my friend Sally Ann told me about the British women who were prisoners of the Japanese in Singapore. The women were part of some slave labor that were building an airport. Now, who knows the why of any behavior, but for reasons best known to themselves, the Japanese soldiers would take some of the women and tie them to stakes in a field and plant bamboo underneath them. That's what I said, so what? But bamboo — I didn't know this — some species of bamboo grows very fast. It grows very tall in a matter of days and the Japs would carefully arrange the women's legs so that the bamboo would grow up in between them. Up, up, up, until the bamboo reached their vaginas. Then they would carefully arrange the flower petals of their vaginas around the bamboo and . . . well, the bamboo just kept on growing. And the fuckin' Japs just sat down on the earth and watched.

After a musical interlude and an intermission, another kabuki drama began. It was the story of an old woman and some warriors who are trying to convert her to Buddhism. They find out that she is a demon, and she tries to devour them, but gradually weakens and dies. Well, the audience went crazy at the end of the performance. There were bravos and bravas and curtain calls and more bravos, but I couldn't even clap, not even once. I wanted to applaud, but all I could think of was those women tied to stakes in some long-forgotten field, waiting for the bamboo to grow.

Biting the Dust
from *Horrible Essays*
by Francine M. Storey

In the end, I have decided that I don't believe in the Tarot cards, and I hate Tanya for giving me the reading, and then insinuating that I was becoming too materialistic. She said I was choosing money over love. I don't believe in love anymore. I'm tired of the supreme effort that it takes to maintain love. I think most people are replaceable. I mean, everyone is saying the same thing today, with no individuality at all, so I began to figure that if I had to listen to the same conversation, I might as well do it on the beach at Acapulco with Chuck, instead of the ghetto at 93rd and Columbus with John.

Now the absolute truth is that I don't care anymore about anything. Even a hint about the whales going extinct leaves me cold, whereas it used to arouse in me a ravenous anger, and I wanted to dash off to Iceland and Africa and bomb all the whaling stations. But who can stop them? Who can stop the oil mongers and the ocean killers? Who can? Not me. I feel powerless over them. Just as I feel powerless trying to get John to leave his wife. I realized in that gloomy October that John would never, never leave his wife, and I gave up. Gave up in the worst way, because I, a former Las Vegas showgirl, had lost out to a big, fat, ugly moo cow woman. I just can't understand it. It goes against nature. Everyone knows that the beautiful woman always seduces the husband away from the frumpy housewife. But not me. I have lost the most fundamental battle, and I hate it a lot.

The Singer
by Chocolate Waters

She lives in the apartment below me. At least I think she lives there. I have never actually seen her. Maybe just her voice lives there, and she moved out years ago. In New York, no one knows the difference, as long as the rent is paid.

The Singer has several unusual styles of singing, depending on how late at night it is, how depressed she is, or how drunk she is. None of her styles depend on whether or not I want to listen to her. In her '60s Rock Band mode, she imagines she's Janis Joplin. Unfortunately, she's more off-key than Janis ever was, and she needs about two more quarts of Southern Comfort. Or maybe I need two more quarts. In her Contemporary Pop mode, she turns into Liza Minnelli and Twisted Sister: "If I can make it there, I'll make it anywhere. It's up to you, New York, New York," she screams. I open the window, "So make it already and move to another building!" In her Judy Collins mode, she can actually sing. At least she does it quietly enough to make me think so.

There's an older man who goes in and out of her apartment. He looks like John Gotti. My kinder self says, maybe he's her father. I wish he was John Gotti. Then he could throw us all a party, and I'd be so busy eating steak, I wouldn't care if she sang or not.

To tell the truth, I think I met her the other day, because she was with that man who looks like John Gotti. Our eyes locked momentarily. "The Singer?" I asked tentatively. She nodded her head in agreement. "I live in the apartment just above you." "Ahhh," she nodded knowingly, "The Writer."

Psychic
by Jeanie Columbo

I went to the Gypsy Tea Room to see Maisie, who's a psychic. It's like ten dollars to go there for fifteen minutes. So I went, really to find out about my play and how it was going to be received and what was going to happen. And so I went there, I paid the guy ten dollars, and I sat down to talk to her, and I said to her, "Almost a year ago, you had said that I would write something, and I didn't believe you, because I've never written anything before. And you told me that like in January, and the next August I wrote a play for no reason other than this dance studio closed, and it meant a lot to everybody, and we all missed it, and I decided to write about it. And now we have a production coming up, and because you were so right on about me writing, I wanted to find out how the play was going to be received."

And so she said . . . the first thing she said was, "Uncross your legs." I was like, "Oh, okay." I guess that had something to do with it. I don't know. Is that too weird? And then she said, "Is your lover in this play?" And I said, "Yes," and so she said, "Yes, yes, I can see that, and I can see that you've lost friendships." And I said, "Yes, that's true, we lost a director, but we're friendly now. And two friends, you know, one of them dropped out of the play, but I'm not angry about it."

So she said, "But this thing with your lover, now what's his name?" And I started to say her name, I started to say . . . Well, I didn't want to tell her that it was a woman, so I said, "His name is Den . . ." And I couldn't think of a name, so I stopped there. I said "Den," because I couldn't . . . I was too embarrassed to tell her that my lover's name was Denise. So she said, "His name is Den?" So I said, "Den, that's his name." I was too frightened, even, to say Dennis or think up anything. It was like my mind was a blank, 'cause I was lying. And then she said, "Well . . ." and she went on to ask about his children. She said, "Well there are a lot of . . . how many children does he have?" And I said, "A lot, but they're not really children." And she said, "I see one that's eighteen." And I said, "Well, that was a little girl that I raised, who's eighteen." And I was like, "My God, she knows Lydia's age." And she said, "So these are all his former, you know, loves?" And I said, "Yes." And I thought, "My God, she sees that this person calls all her former lovers her children, because she felt so motherly."

And then I realized that every time she said "his" or "him," she would put an emphasis on it, like she knows that I lied, and then I realized that she knows Lydia is eighteen, and she knows all these people that Den considers children are lovers, she's gotta know that Den's a woman and that I lied to a psychic, because I'm too embarrassed to tell her the truth, but she probably knows it anyway.

My friend Louise told me that she's going to go back to see Maisie, maybe on Good Friday, and she said that I should go with her and just tell her the truth, and I said, "What for, she already knows. She's just going to say, 'This is the one that thinks she's lying to me'."

Warpath Vocabulary
by Madeline Miller

Oh, yes, I knew what it meant. But when a woman I used to play cards with said it out loud, I nearly fell off my chair from shock. I thought that she was a lady.

That's what my parents would have said. You see, I was brought up to be a lady. I was taught to abide by their old-world rules. After each meal, it was a ritual of saying "thank you" and kissing their hands. Anyone older than I was addressed as Aunt and Uncle. "Please" and "thank you" were taken for granted. I don't remember all the serious offenses, but my parents threatened to send me to a boarding school in Switzerland to learn good manners, if I broke any of the house rules. I don't know why they picked Switzerland. It could have been Japan, where people bow to each other all the time.

Growing up in New York City, it's easy to hear all the taboo words. I've learned them all, and apply one or more to passersby who bump me, or drivers who don't let me cross the street. See, I've had it. I'm on the warpath. All you bullies beware. I'm fighting back.

Take the kids today. You know, teenagers hanging around the street corner. It starts even younger, though. When my best girlfriend's four-year-old, Kevin, was left in my charge, so she could go to her beauty parlor, I almost passed out from shock. Evidently, little Kevin was displeased about something. Right in the middle of the gutter, while crossing the street and I'm holding his little chubby hand, with his little manly voice, he shouted, "You cunt!" Somehow we got to the other side. Quietly and ladylike, I asked him, "Where did you hear that, Kevin?" He answered willingly, "My Fadder said it to my Mudder."

I'm not really proud of it, talking this way, but

sometimes I'm caught off guard, especially in the street. People do a double-take, when they see a woman who looks like a lady and has a foul mouth. It pays off, too, when I suspect the danger of being mugged. I just open my mouth and spew out all the worst words I know. Nobody bothers me. I'm not a lady.

An Evening in Helsinki
by Ida Barron

It was common knowledge where I was brought up, in the Lower East Side of Manhattan, that girls who were not careful — who took candy from strange men — were in danger of being kidnapped by "white slavers" who would send them to brothels in Rio de Janeiro. That last phrase was said in lowered tones. The idea was intriguing, but I didn't dwell on it and even forgot about it — until the summer I went to Europe with my friend Joyce, and we landed eventually in Helsinki, Finland.

On the train to the city, we met a very nice Finnish man. He spoke German, I spoke a select Yiddish. He said his name was Neel, and that he was a school teacher. So were Joyce and I, so we felt like kindred spirits, even without much language. He told us he would pick us up at our hotel that evening and show us Helsinki. We agreed. Afterward Joyce, bubbly and funny, said, "How exciting! Maybe he's a white slaver!" We laughed.

Neel — that's what his name sounded like — arrived on time and in a nice car. We got in. He drove off. We passed through the lively part of town and reached a neighborhood that looked like nighttime warehouse neighborhoods in New York. Quiet. Dark. Deserted. Scary. "White slaver," Joyce whispered. We giggled, but I suddenly remembered the things my mother told me.

The car pulled up at one of the darkened buildings. Neel got out, and we followed, putting on a brave front, but beginning to wonder if we were idiots. Inside, we followed Neel down a long, dark corridor, turned a few times into other long, dark corridors. Joyce and I looked at each other. This time we both mouthed "white slaver." What else could it be?

Finally, we stopped at a door. It opened. Neel ushered us in. Here we were, two somewhat bedraggled tourists, not exactly giggling anymore, but game.

Well, will you believe this? The room was a large, well-lit cabaret with a band up front and people sitting at small tables eating, drinking, enjoying in a nice way. Down the center was a red carpet, really and truly. And we were apparently expected. As we walked down that red carpet with Neel, people applauded, and the band played what they seemed to think was the American national anthem — "Turkey in the Straw."

All in our honor, for which we didn't even have to fight, after all. We had a wonderful time, but Joyce being Joyce, wondered for years whether we missed something by not going to Rio de Janeiro.

In the Schoolyard
by Alan Stolzer

The schoolyard fence didn't support him. It sagged as he leaned against it. And though the darkening day tasted of winter, naturally, he wasn't dressed properly. My mother tried looking after him, but a threadbare, leather windbreaker was all he let his diminished body bear. Besides, he wasn't aware of the cold or anything else. His eyes focused on me alone.

I hadn't seen him for awhile, and I ran toward him, a happy and innocent ten-year-old. I'd have jumped into his arms or challenged him to a race, but the nearer I got, the more I realized I was bigger now, and somehow, he was smaller. But something more had changed. He never looked this bad, no matter what. I wanted to ask if everything was all right, but I knew he wouldn't answer. He wanted something else.

I could see a rash that came and went on his neck and hands, and I knew he'd be scratching it, as furiously as he shouldn't have. Why wouldn't he use the salve my mother got him? Then I saw them — my parents — down the block. What were they doing here? Surely they hadn't come for me — I'd be home soon. They held back, nervous, reluctant to approach. He didn't notice them. As I said, he looked at me and nothing else.

The cold was biting him. I could tell how uncomfortable he was. And that rash, always spreading, always there. How many tears did my mother shed? His problems forever criss-crossed, ravaging him to distraction.

He'd spotted them. Incapable of being furtive, my parents came closer, and he saw them. My father, reluctant, held back, but my mother forced herself forward. His gaze swung from me to them for the first time. I saw my father glance over his shoulder at a white truck, a small one, moving slowly beside them. At first, I thought it was an ice cream seller, but summer was over, and now, even I could see it was an ambulance.

My mother stopped, maybe twenty feet away. Her body shook, sobbing as I'd never seen her sob. He began walking toward her, and just as quickly, my father came to her side. Two men got out of the truck. My uncle stopped. As my mother sagged into my father's arms, he turned to me, hair blown about, mouth open.

I heard my mother yell for me to leave. I turned obediently, then heard her muffling her cries. I turned around and saw him moving toward my parents, but before he reached them, the two men cut him off. My mother touched his arm as they took him. I watched until the truck turned the corner. The schoolyard concrete had gotten very cold.

Beginning My Twenties
by Peter DeMarco

It's like all hospital waiting rooms. I'm sitting on a cheap vinyl couch. My father lies somewhere beyond the swinging Emergency Room door to my right. Faceless white blurs scurry around like bugs beneath an upturned rock.

I'm crying so hard the tears are dripping on my mud-caked construction work boots. There's a muddy mess on the floor in front of me. I feel a hand. The nurse tries to look compassionate, asking me to sign something on a clipboard. Just another day at the office, practicing the art of saving lives before lunch.

She disappears through those swinging doors. I'm left alone with my prayers. But what good are prayers? Dad prayed every day of his goddamn life, and it didn't keep Mom from dying. And now the poor bastard himself was hanging on by a thread. I thought he was the healthiest guy in the world. What do you have to do to stay alive on this fucking planet? Only the good die young, it seems, while miserable drunk slobs like my Aunt Lou waste away on couches across America.

The nurse comes back and motions for me to follow. I walk down the hall. The sounds fade to a faint whisper, like a radio that's turned down so low you're not even sure if it's on. I go into a room where a bland-faced doctor makes me sit.

"Your father expired eight minutes ago," a mechanical voice says.

It's a hell of a way to begin my twenties.

Chain Reaction
by Garrison Phillips

You ever watch a column of ants? They have this uncanny, instant communication, and if you nudge one ant with your foot or a stick, all of a sudden the whole column knows, and there's a chain reaction. That's how it seemed to me on a weekend trip last spring with my hiking group. It was as though we wove a silent web of love and support for and around our friend with AIDS. We didn't plan it. We didn't talk about it. And it wasn't like it was a showy thing. It simply was. Saturday night, we all gathered wood and helped lay the fire, but we let him light it. He said grace at supper, and he had asked us to not bow our heads. He said he wanted everyone to look at him while he said thanks. To really look at him and forget about the lesions that marked his face and neck. And then in his grace, he said thanks for his friends. At breakfast Sunday morning, I sat opposite him at the very end of the last table, and we talked. Talked a little about how he felt, about the weather, about the day's outing.

That afternoon, we rendezvoused in our usual parking lot at the park. It was clouding over, but still bright, as we began our goodbyes and packed hiking gear into our cars. He was standing there, so small and still, with his parka hood pulled up over his head, saying goodbye to various guys — surrounded by friends, yet somehow alone in a crowd of people. Looking at him, with his peaked hood shadowing his deep set eyes, I was reminded of all the nameless saints of church windows and renaissance paintings. I went to him and put my arms around him to hug him goodbye. I just wanted to hold him. To let him know that I cared about him, wished him better, prayed for a safe journey ahead. And that's when it happened. Suddenly all of us were floating high up at the tops of the trees. I could see my back and my friend's face hugged into my shoulder. I was looking down on all of us from a great height, but yet I could see us from below suspended above the parking lot. It was like being in a room, yet seeing all sides at the same time — both inside and out, and from above and below. The cars were floating, too, and we were all holding hands right through them. Not through open doors and windows, but right through the cars, like they were mist or smoke. All of us holding hands and laughing. And then other friends of mine were there holding hands, too. Princey and Jodie and Raul and Charlie. Laughing and holding hands in a big circle with the wind in our faces as we danced — danced over the treetops.

And then it was over, and I was kind of shaking, standing in the parking lot, my arms around my friend. What had happened? How much time had passed. I felt a shudder of panic. Had anyone else seen what I had seen? Was I okay? But everyone seemed the same. Goodbyes were still being said, car doors slamming, guys yelling, "Safe home," "Drive carefully." I realized that I had seen all that in an instant, and nothing had actually changed. But it's an image I can never forget.

Panama City
by John Woodson

I was in Panama City, Florida, staying in a concrete motel painted pink with a real, live palm tree out the window and a small, bitter beach out back, where they had a picnic table. I sat out there with my shirt off most of the afternoon, sipping on a few cold ones. Later, I get dressed and go out looking, I'm thinking, for some food, when I find this concrete bunker of a bar, and in I walk. They had the bar in the middle of this place, made out of glass brick with blue lights inside it. And the bartender, turns out was also the owner, had his chief petty officer uniform all pressed and sealed in plastic, like when it comes out of the dry cleaners, hanging smack above the bar in the dead center for all to see, with his medals and decorations and everything. He still looked like what a chief petty officer should look like: buzz cut, barrel-chested, belly hanging out, but strong, with two big tattoos on his forearms, one of a naked woman in high heels, sort of 1940ish, and the other arm, I think it was the right, had a painting of a ship, long ways. Well, he was real nice, and he told me all 'bout his career in the Navy for about twenty minutes. Then I bought a round.

Sitting on the other side of this bar was an older woman, good-looking, maybe twice my age, but had the nicest legs, and she would get off her stool and go play the juke box, one song at a time. She was wearing a slinky blue dress, and you could tell she still had firm, big titties. Well, I offered to stake her to the juke box, if she'd join me for a drink, which she did. And she was a looker up close, too, and after awhile I think, I am going to get lucky with this hot momma. She is going to show me some things, and I am going to rejuvenate her with my youth. Well, 'bout that time, my euphoria was

33

interrupted by this old guy who looked like what I think Kit Carson looked like, asking me if he could buy me, us, a drink. So now Kit Carson and I are in this conversation, when I notice my hot momma is at another table, and Kit Carson is telling me he is the last surviving member of Al Capone's gang, and he was in prison for three years, got out and been living off this money Big Al put away for the gang members. And it looked like I didn't believe him, so he reaches down, and he's wearing this short boot, the kind my uncle wore when he was drivin' semis across the country, and he pulls out a little .22 pistol. And he asks me again if I believe him, wavin' this little gun in my face 'bout one foot away, when the petty officer grabs me and ushers me out the door, and me saying, "I didn't do nothing," and he saying, "Don't be stupid, go on." And later I think I came a foot away from dying, and I didn't even know it. I completely forgot 'bout my older woman in the blue dress, too.

The Great White Dope
by Richard Roy

The guy I fought for the title was Big Jim Mitchel. This guy hit ya, he'd knock ya inta the middle of next week. We fought at Madison Square Garden. Place was sold out. So I'm in my dressing room before the fight, trying to keep loose. Man, I was scared as hell. Finally, I get the knock on the door. Fight time. So I'm makin' my way to the ring. I'm walkin' down that long, dark corridor. You could see the ring in the distance, hear the roar of the crowd. I get into the ring, this guy had a face like a pit bull. I mean, he was ugly. So the first round, I come out and pop him three times in the nose. Guy starts bleeding. By the third round, I had him right where I wanted him. I come out, fake him one to the gut, hook him to the body, overhand right, BANG! Broke his nose. Blood all over the place. I . . .

I'm trying to finish him off. The ref had ta pull me off him . . . pull me off him. But the biggest thrill, I'm leavin' the Garden, I'm takin' pictures with people, I'm shakin' hands, I kissed a baby. But the biggest thrill, right there on Seventh Avenue, on the ticker tape, it said, "WIN 3 ROUNDS, KNOCK OUT, HOLLYWOOD ROY, NEW! HEAVYWEIGHT CHAMPION OF THE WORLD."

Of the world. I like it.

Breasts
by Roger Cacchiotti

I'm not sure when I grew breasts, but in Junior High School, when I realized I had them, I wished I would die. Nobody could call me fat. Chunky maybe, but certainly not fat enough to be grossly out of shape. Yet, I had breasts that competed with most of the girls in high school. What bothers me most is, I never noticed them until a handsome, muscular guy pinched them in gym class, saying I was bigger and felt better than his girlfriend, making all the guys roar with laughter. Before long, the guys would caress and pinch my breasts whenever they saw me. This happened everywhere — in the hallways, in math class, in art class and even at the dances. My shoulders curled forward in hopes of hiding them, making my neck and upper back look like a camel. No matter what I wore, I couldn't camouflage my breasts, so my arms became permanently crossed.

My life changed dramatically with the discovery of my breasts. Elementary school friends who I had known almost all my life began walking to school by different routes. Once I found them walking together on a side street, and I yelled out, "Hey, guys, wait up," but they began running when they saw me. And I realized the truth: they were embarrassed about my breasts.

In gym class, the guys never picked me while choosing sides for sporting events, so eventually the coach made one team take me. I never cried. Just stood there in total panic. I never hit the ball or caught the ball or even knew whether it was a ball or a puck. All I knew was to stand in a certain way so the guys wouldn't see my breasts. Sometimes during half time, a bunch of the guys would gang around me, knock me down on the ground, lift up my T-shirt, pinch me, slap me and scream with hysteria, making my chest hot pink. The coach would make them stop, but he always let them do it first. Although I hated their teasing, a part of me liked their attention.

But I couldn't take it. I felt like a freak. So I skipped gym class for a month and then, of course, was suspended from school — the coach caught me in the library, hiding behind a stack of books.

But even though my grades dropped as the year progressed and I hardly went to school — I was out "sick" a lot — I did manage to get into college. After my first year of college, my father sent me to Hawaii for a vacation. My first plane ride. I loved Hawaii. Best of all, nobody knew me. I still had those breasts, but Hawaiian shirts covered them well. During my stay on the islands, I bought some diet pills and managed to lose forty pounds of what my father called baby fat. Starvation and rigorous exercise seemed delightful after years of shame in school.

Before I jumped into my morning shower at the end of the summer, I caught a glimpse of my naked body, something I usually avoided. There in the mirror, right in front of me, was a 170-pound man with no female breasts. They had melted away. I stood there and cried, touching my chest, touching my thin body, thanking God for this long-prayed-for miracle.

I wore my Hawaiian shirt out on the beach and then slowly removed it, as if unveiling a statue. There I stood with my naked chest. Nobody noticed me. Nobody looked at me. It was wonderful. I ran around the beach, jumped into the water, rubbing my body with the warm water, which was glistening in the hot sun.

It has been fifteen years since I lost my breasts. Yet sometimes when I see a young, handsome boy with a flat and muscular chest, I can still hear the laughter from so many years ago.

Lessons About Luv
by Howard Katz Fireheart

I was living with a woman on the Upper West Side. She was a hippie type. Echo was not at fault when she . . . well, you see, we had a party, or I had a party. It was my birthday, it was her birthday, it was a big deal. I could finally get the loft I always wanted. She was just "trying to teach us all a lesson about luv."

I told her the guy who's throwing the party's got $5,000 for me to get me started. But he's also my friend, kinda, and so I guess she must have thought that meant it was a party, like an all-out, sloppy, dead-and-grateful, invite-who-you-want, everything's hippy, dippy, trippy party.

So, I had a neighbor. I say that politely, because I hope if he hears this and can remember me out of a drunken stupor, he'll think kindly of me and won't track me down. Well, we were living in a welfare hotel, La Bell Nord, in lovely eight-by-ten rooms with three-foot hallways. And oh, did I forget to mention this Puerto Rican gentleman had just gotten out of jail for the unfortunate demise of a colleague by his hand? The long and short: she invited him. I said, "He's nasty when he gets drunk." She said, "He's my friend, and you're mean. You uninvite him." She told him I was prejudiced, and that's why he couldn't come to the party. I mean, this girl grew up in Ohio; she was white bread.

So let's play "Guess What Happened."

Let's not.

I stayed at a friend's for the next three days, leaving the room vulnerable, but life, limb and plan intact, for now.

The night of the event, she's there all in white lace and $3 feather boa, slightly pouty. I'm a little nervous, but okay. Well, let me explain. The loft he lives in is a one-room palace, and the kitchen's open. I'm social. There's a crowd gathering around a hysterical figure sliding and writhing down the fridge moaning, "He was my friend. Now you've ruined my birthday, too."

I'm dizzy watching the money pass away. The guy's wife freaks out consoling my little Echo. "Shit! Who's this guy we're giving five grand to?"

A hazy, red color, then fade-out.

Next day, back in my lovely eight-by-ten room, bang! I am wakened gently to the sound of my neighbor pounding on my door, uncomfortably close to my head, and in the background, the rustling of a fellow creature, Mr. Rat, and a gunshot. Shit!

The Cowboy
from *Playing Movies*
by Ruth Brandeis

You say everybody's got dreams? Well, I didn't. I didn't have time for things like that. I had to take care of myself. My father died when I was fifteen, and I had to borrow money to bury him. I got a full-time job, finished high school, and then went to college. I kept the apartment I lived in with my father — a one-room hole with the bathroom down the hall. Now, they call these places "studios."

I never told you, but when I was much younger, I lived on a farm. My father got a job as a cook on this very large farm, and since I was the help's kid, I lived in a cabin on the grounds by myself. My father did more drinking with his buddies than he did cooking.

I guess I was lonely. I didn't know it until later on. Lots of times, I had no one to talk to. When it got real bad, I'd jump on this old mare they kept on the farm. They didn't let me use the saddle, so I'd jump on her bareback, and every day she'd run back to the barn, and every day I'd fall off her. I loved that old mare. Her name was Misty, and when I rode her, I felt great, like a hero or something.

Okay, okay, I wanted to be a cowboy. After awhile, I'd be able to ride Misty for a couple of hours at a time, and I used to picture myself like Gary Cooper,* coming to the rescue of homesteaders and having women fall in love with me, because I was so strong. Some days, I'd put on a black shirt and a black cowboy hat and carry a toy pistol — some of them looked pretty real — and Misty and I would ride up the mountain, and I'd picture myself riding off into the sunset. I'm always alone, but it's okay, because like Gary Cooper, I'm a man who's comfortable with myself and whatever comes. I'd even talk to my horse, and she seemed to understand that I was a man in charge of my own destiny — just like a real cowboy.

* Younger actors may substitute Clint Eastwood

The Ice Cream Strategy
from *Reunion at Red Fork*
by Jerry E. McGee

Red Fork is not without crime. Oh, yeah, we had a shoplifter at the store. Must have been, what, 1968? There was this old gal used to come from Alma about once a month. She'd shop around, buy a few of the specials, and after every time she'd been there, we'd find a few things were missing. So, this one time, in the middle of the summer, she was in there shopping, so I kind of kept an eye on her. She went over to the freezer, one of those old ones where you lift the rubber top off and reach down into it. She set her purse down in the freezer and dug around in the ice cream for a flavor. In the middle of the digging, I thought I saw her put a pint of ice cream in her purse, then she looked around some more, and finally decided not to buy anything. She took her purse out, closed up the lid and angled her way toward the front door. So I waited till she went outside, and then I stepped out, too.

"Hey," I said, "I won't keep you but a minute, but I wanted to ask you about something." And I started to talk to her. I don't even remember what I talked about, just whatever I could think of. And she was trying to cut me off and make it to her car. And I kept talking to her. In those days, ice cream came in those square boxes that were folded, sort of like Chinese food containers, and they held frozen ice cream all right, but when it started to melt, look out, they leaked like crazy.

I talked to her and I talked to her. It was the hottest day of summer, must have been a hundred degrees out there, and I knew that stuff was leaking in her purse and running all over everything. She knew it, too, and there wasn't anything she could do about it. She was trying to figure out if I knew she'd taken something. I never accused her of a thing. I just kept talking to her.

Your Dad was kind of provoked with me, out there wasting time. He'd call me in, and I'd wave him off and keep talking to her. And she was getting antsy, and she was getting red, and she was getting mad, but there wasn't anything she could do about it.

Finally, when I figured her purse was soup, I said, "Well, I'd better get back to work. Been nice talking to you," and came in the store. She high-tailed it to her car and drove away, real fast. She never came back, to buy anything or to steal anything. You know what your Dad did when I told him why I'd been talking to her? He gave me a raise.

Dimitri

from *A Dream of Del Monte*

by Brother Augustine Towey, CM

The first thing is — and I'm telling you, because you always said you liked her — the first thing is that it was my fault. I mean, I've been working here two-and-a-half, going on three years now, and like I know the stock, and I know where the stock goes — I mean the shelves — like it was the shelves in my own house. And I know you're fussy about them, like it was your own house. Like you tell us, think of the Mart like your home, which is because we're here so much. And I mean, I like the overtime, Mr. Nasdropolos, I'm not complaining. God forbid you should take this as a complaint and fire me, too, even though you'd have grounds, because, like I'm saying, it's my fault. I gave her charge of aisle four to eight, and she came to us, you gotta remember, which I didn't, with no experience, and she's nervous-like. She isn't dumb, which it looks. I think it's nervous.

What she did, and her mistake, was she took the twenty-eight cans of red-labeled sweet peas from the third shelf and put them on the second shelf near the twelve cans of green-labeled whole kernel corn. Which was sort of okay, because I had moved the twenty-four cans of no-name white-label lentils across the aisle near the Del Monte lentils, where there was room. And then she moved the no-name black olives in the space on the third shelf, which she had vacated when she moved the twenty-eight cans of red-labeled sweet peas. This left the no-name green olives next to the Libby's black olives, being a gap like — I mean, if you look at the shelf, it's kind of funny-looking.

But I think her mistake was in taking the eighteen cans of asparagus tips from the fifth aisle and putting them in the seventh aisle next to the thirty-two jars of

Vlasic dills. I can understand the black olives — it's natural — but the pickles don't make sense. So she filled the space for the asparagus tips with twenty-one canisters of Kraft Parmesan and eighteen canisters of Parmesan-Romano. That's when I came in. Right away I saw what she did. I saw the parmesan and the parmesan-romano and the olives and the pickles. So I tried to rectify the situation, which was a real haste-makes-waste, which was when you came in. That's when you saw the Pampers. That wasn't her, Mr. Nasdropolos, that was me. I put the Pampers next to the olives.

No Apology Necessary
from *It's About Time*
by Dennis Sook

You have forgotten my name — I can tell by the look on your face. Well, no apology necessary, Della. It's very understandable. Let me explain. We just met. I've obviously not made a strong enough impression for you to remember my name. But I'm not insulted. I'll look on the bright side and consider this to be a challenge. My name is "Barber." Joe Barber. It rhymes with "barber," as in haircuts. But that is not my means of livelihood. I don't mess with hair. I am not a barber. I have nothing against barbers, but by the same token, I have nothing for barbers either. Kind of a stupid profession, really. Why would a human being want to cut his hair? Much less someone else's hair. I mean, the God that created us all, in his infinite wisdom, made the conscious decision to strategically insert and imbed hair follicles in specific areas. For example, not on the palms of your hands or on the palms of your feet. No hair follicles on your tongue. But other areas. Let it grow. Full-bodied and rich and free-flowing. Lustrous, lively and long hair. But, back to the real question — do you remember my name?

Performance
Pieces

Sharon
by Heide Arbitter

This town's stuffed with people. You can meet anybody at any time, and nobody's got to be lonely. But even when I ain't washing and drying in this cellar, I don't meet nobody, most of the time, so I'm looking forward to talking about it. So I wait for the bus thirty-five minutes, and I'm late, 'cause I had twelve extra loads to scrub, and I'm getting nervous. So I take a bite of the sandwich I've been carrying around since lunch, when a guy hanging around smiles at me. Me! And I think I remember him, but all he says is, "What kind of sandwich is that?"

Well, it's cream cheese and olives, of course, and I ask him if he wants to share. He says, "No," but his eyes say, "Yes." So I tell him, "I got it in Marcy's, the rip-off joint that refuses to make donations." Now he looks like he's starving, and I try to think, 'Is this guy's name John, Jim, Tim, Hamilton or what?'

"You're from the neighborhood," he says. He don't remember my name either. He's drooling, so I offer him half the sandwich, and again he says, "No." But now his hands are rubbing circles on his fat stomach, and I can tell he wants to fill it with me.

"Take it. Take it all," I say, handing him the whole thing, cause it finally dawns on me his name is Jim. "You know, Jim, we've had a date."

Well, Jim tells me he doesn't remember, but that I shouldn't take it personal, and he polishes off seven dollars and eighty-six cents in one bite.

I'm so embarrassed, I try getting a cab, and I'm about to climb in, when the bus gets here. I jump onto the bus. The cab driver curses me in Italian, I think, and I crawl to the back of the bus. But Jim takes the last seat and says, "I got a date with a mermaid. We're eating at Crab's Fish Joint across the street from the docks. I hope she's the understanding type, 'cause I'm a little late."

I tell him, "I got a date, too. I got an appointment with my shrink. His office is in the renovated warehouse on top of Crab's. He knows I'm late, but he's waiting for me anyway." And when we finally get to the docks, Jim runs out of the bus shouting, "This time I won't forget you."

"My name's Sharon!" I yell to Jim, but he's already through the revolving door. And as I pass Crab's, I see through the window that Jim's mermaid is chowing down with another guy.

So I walk into the warehouse, and I'm alone as I get in the elevator and press six. The doors are closing, as a bald guy carrying rubber hoses runs in. He presses eight and stares at the floor. 'He's shy, too,' I think. Then he looks me direct in the eyes, then back down at the floor. "Um," he begins, "I love your stockings." I look down at my shoes. I'm wearing ordinary black stockings. "Do you got a thing for nuns?" I ask. And you know what he answered? He asked if I was a nun! "Your stockings are beautiful," he says. "Where did you get them?"

"Woolworth's," I answer.

The elevator stops on six, but the door doesn't open.

"What the hell?" I say.

"Don't say 'hell'," he whispers.

He pushes on the door. It doesn't open. I press the alarm. It doesn't go off. I'm about to start screaming, when he says, "I bought a thousand pounds of marshmallows. I'm setting up a stand, outside the firehouse on Green Street, so I can sell roasted marshmallows to the firemen. It's going to be a cold, cold winter."

"It's only July," I say.

"My marshmallows will keep you warm," he answers. He pushes eight. As we get out, he warns, "Don't say 'hell,' and I'll see you in Woolworth's. Goodbye, Miss Nun." He opens the door to an apartment, and I hear his mother scream, "Vinny, I've baked you a sausage, fit for a king!"

"This is why I talk to a shrink," I say, but Vinny's already slammed the door in my face. So I walk down two flights, and I knock on the door. At last Dr. Sludge opens it. His office is lit with candles. He looks annoyed.

"Sharon, you didn't get my message. You should talk to your secretary more often." I tell Dr. Sludge I don't have a secretary. He continues, "I have to cancel. This is the first time in three months that Cindy's been able to get away from her husband. We just started hors d'oeuvres. I'll see you next week."

He locks the door. I walk six floors to the street. The cop on the corner ignores me, as he guzzles Gatorade, and now I got to wait for the bus again. But there's no bus in sight, and nobody's waiting either. I'm hungry, so I take chewing gum from my pocket. It's full of lint. I swallow the gum, along with the lint. Forty minutes later, the bus pulls in.

"I don't understand this town," I say to the driver. "When I came out, the bus was jammed. Now I'm going home, and it's empty."

"Don't blame me," he snaps, as he stuffs his mouth with potato chips. I think of asking for one, but don't get around to it, 'cause he throws the empty cellophane on the floor, and we continue across town in silence, and not one passenger gets on. At my stop, I jump off and run all the way to Marcy's. I relax as I step inside. I walk up and down the aisles looking at cans of peas and frozen pizzas and boxes of cookies. It feels like I'm with my mother.

"Weren't you here before?" Marcy asks, 'cause she remembers me. "I'm closing in five minutes."

"Cream cheese and olives on white bread," I tell her. "You're the only one I allow to spot up my white, so be careful to lay those little green slices and red dots of pimento just right."

"You would ask me to lay down the olives, when my hemorrhoids are falling off and I'm trying to go home." But she places out two slices of white bread and spreads on a thin layer of cream cheese, just the way I like it. She cuts a few olives in half and lays them out very artistically with their pimentos. She charges me nine dollars, and I leave. Then she locks the door and turns on the alarm.

"Rip-off joint!" I scream, but Marcy doesn't hear.

I get to my building. A homeless guy and his dalmatian are sorting through a garbage can. I go up to my kitchen, but I've lost my appetite. I get two glasses from the dirty ones in the sink. I fill them with water. I open the bag from Marcy's and take out the sandwich. I'm still not hungry, so I put the sandwich on a plate. I carry the sandwich and the water downstairs. It's 11 p.m., and as I watch the guy and his dalmatian eat, I see that charity is the fastest way to companionship.

The Long Black Wall
by John Woodson

I remember, it was a spring day, and I was lying in my bed, which was in the garage at the time, and my mother came in and said they had just dedicated this long, black wall to all the vets, and why don't I come in and see what it looks like on the news. So I did, and sat and watched with a Bud. This reporter talked about how all the names of everyone who was there, or something, was written on the wall. And Momma said, "Then your name's in Washington, our nation's capitol." And also that reporter said that all the guys who died or MIA'd were on it also, and I thought of a couple of fellas.

So later that night, after thinking about it, I told the old man and Momma that I was going to go to Washington to see if that reporter was right and look for my name on this black wall and look for some other names. Momma thought it was a good idea for me to get out of the house, since I ain't been nowhere in a long time, and the old man just laughed. Thought I was crazy, and it was another excuse to not work and spend his hard-earned money. And no, he wouldn't let me use the car or give me a goddamn dime. I said, "That's alright. I can hitch, and I don't need money. I got my disability check." And he said he's been cashing that to take out for food and rent and my beer, and I told him I wanted to see my bank book. I should have several thousand dollars in that bank book. He just laughed. Said I drank it all and spent it on rent, and I got mad and had to go outside. The dark, for some reason, calms me and makes me feel better.

Momma came out after a bit, after the old man yelled at her, and she gave me this envelope and told me not to look in it. Just put it in my jacket, and maybe I better go now and not wait till the morning, 'cause the old man was in rare form and might do something. And I kissed her on the cheeks, and she held me and told me good luck finding my name and others, and write when I did — I was still her little boy. So I had on my fatigue jacket and jeans and a T-shirt and this envelope. I walked away from Momma's house into the dark and hitched a ride to St. Louis, where I got me a bus ticket to Washington. That envelope had 178 dollars in it. I put fifty of it in one of those lockers at the bus depot. I still got the key around my neck.

I am not sure how long that bus took to get to Washington, but it was a day or so, and when I got to that wall, there were lots of people there doing all sort of the same thing I was doing there. Lots of mothers, but also guys. Some were leaving their Zippos on the ground next to the wall, and there were these noncoms in uniform asking what name I wanted. But I didn't trust them. I figured out the names were listed in the year you started your tour, so I went and found my name, and then I started seeing others that I recognized, till I found the platoon. Well, I spent the night and next day there, and the next night, for some reason, and I hadn't slept, really, or eaten. And every day and night, people came there, and I thought that this was a good thing, and that reporter wasn't lying. And I decided I would stay by the wall for awhile, and maybe some of my buddies would come around, or some of the officers, and we could all talk, maybe, or go get a beer together.

Then the next day, this Marine in full dress stops me, saying he's noticed I been here every day and night for awhile, and what was I doing. And I tell him, I am looking for names and looking to see if anyone finds my name, and then I would know them. And he says my name can't be on there. And I tell him it is and show it to him, and he says I should wait and goes way. He comes back with this Army officer lieutenant, and he asks me some questions and wants to see my discharge papers, and I tell him they are back home with Momma, and asks me what unit and when I was in and really starts giving me the third degree. And the Marine sees I am getting tense and tells me it's okay, he just wants to help.

And then the Army lieutenant wants me to follow him so he can do a test. I don't like any of this, and I start to walk away, but they keep talking to me. Then they are shouting and start to order me, and I say I am no longer in the fucking show, and they have no right. And the Army lieutenant grabs me, and I shove him down, and that Marine gives me a punch and tells me to calm down, when they were the ones getting excited. And I push him down, and I walk away, wishing it was dark, cause I need to feel calm. And then I hear sirens, and I don't know why. I start to run, and from behind, I hear some voices shout. And I run harder, till I run into darkness and feel calmer and there were no more shouts, and I sit down by a tree.

I try to figure out what they were talking about my name not being on the wall, so I figure I am going to stay with the wall for awhile and prove that it is there. And maybe some of my buddies will come around, and maybe a few of the good officers will come around, and we can all get a drink together or something. I hear the wall may travel. Maybe I'll go along, see where it goes. Maybe it is looking for some of the names on there.

Scenes

Sylvia & Howard
from *Breakfast*
by Richard Sutherlin

SYLVIA. Do you like these Reeboks, Howard? Tell me the truth.

HOWARD. Mm hmm. They're fine.

SYLVIA. I dreamed about these shoes last night. I wonder what that means? I dreamed that I got ready for work. I put on this suit, then I painted my toe nails bright red and put on a very vulgar pair of mesh stockings. And then I put on a pair of shiny, black, seven-inch stiletto heels and wore them to the office.

HOWARD. Mm hmm . . .

SYLVIA. None of the other women in the office would speak to me. The men didn't seem to mind . . .

HOWARD. It's only stress. Anxiety.

SYLVIA. I am so depressed.

HOWARD. About what, darling?

SYLVIA. Oh, everything. Life. Death. Nuclear winter.

HOWARD. You're depressed about nuclear winter?

SYLVIA. Well, it isn't a happy thing, is it?

HOWARD. Don't worry about it.

SYLVIA. You know how I detest cold weather.

HOWARD. You have a fur coat.

SYLVIA. A fur coat is not going to do the trick, Howard. They are talking very cold for a very long time. Years. With the climate as it is, I'm suicidal by February. How will I deal with twelve months of winter?

HOWARD. Maybe you're hypoglycemic.

SYLVIA. I could never survive it. They're not talking "Winter in the Poconos." They're talking Ice Age.

HOWARD. Maybe it won't happen.

SYLVIA. What if it does?

HOWARD. Maybe it won't. Maybe we'll get the greenhouse effect instead. Palm trees on Fifth Avenue. You like the tropics.

SYLVIA. The ice caps will melt.

HOWARD. We'll homestead Antarctica.

SYLVIA. The oceans will overflow. We should never have bought a second-floor apartment. Who's going to buy an underwater co-op?

HOWARD. In Manhattan? Don't worry. We'll find a buyer.

SYLVIA. Fat chance. I told you we shouldn't buy this place. But, oh, no, 'it's such a great deal,' you said. 'We'll make a fortune,' you said. Now we're up to our necks in mortgage payments, and soon we'll be over our heads in salt water.

HOWARD. Worrywart. Worrywart.

SYLVIA. Nothing worries you.

HOWARD. It will be all right.

SYLVIA. How do you know that?

HOWARD. Or it won't. Either way. And that will be all right, too. Even if it isn't all right, then it will become all right, because it will have to be all right, since that is the way it is, and therefore, all right or not, that is the way it was meant to be, and consequently . . .

SYLVIA. Oh, Howard, please! I loathe Zen.

HOWARD. Darling, even if we don't have forever, we have right now.

SYLVIA. That's a comfort, Howard?

HOWARD. And we have each other.

SYLVIA. Yes, that is a comfort.

HOWARD. And we have one more thing.

SYLVIA. What's that?

HOWARD. We have fifteen minutes before we have to leave for work. Tell me again about those stiletto heels.

SYLVIA. Fifteen minutes?

HOWARD. We can do it in ten. And mesh stockings? Like a can-can girl?

SYLVIA. I haven't finished breakfast.

HOWARD. Mangia! Mangia!

SYLVIA. All right, but don't touch my hair.

Johanna & Weston
from *The Fluorescent Room*
by Dennis Horvitz

JOHANNA. What happened? The wagon! What's going on? What is this place? Who are you?

WESTON. I'm Farron Weston, and I'm a doctor.

JOHANNA. A doctor? What do you mean, a doctor?

WESTON. This is going to be a little difficult to explain.

JOHANNA. What is this place? I want to go home!

WESTON. Actually, you're a long way from home.

JOHANNA. Well, where am I?

WESTON. You're in New York City.

JOHANNA. I live in New York City, and this isn't it. Am I dreaming?

WESTON. No, you're not dreaming, you're awake. This is all very real. Do you remember your name?

JOHANNA. Johanna Brooke.

WESTON. Johanna, I would like to ask you a few more questions to see if your memory is intact. Are you married?

JOHANNA. No.

WESTON. And do you have a job?

JOHANNA. Yes, I'm a teacher.

WESTON. What's the last thing you remember, Johanna?

JOHANNA. I was crossing the street and . . . the wagon! They couldn't stop the wagon! Was I hit?

WESTON. No, you weren't hit. You were pulled to safety.

JOHANNA. What kind of room is this, anyway?

What kind of gas lantern is that? I can't see a flame.

WESTON. That's because there is none.

JOHANNA. A lantern with no flame?

WESTON. Yes. It's called a fluorescent light. It's lit by electricity.

JOHANNA. By what? Light comes from gas lamps. What am I doing here?

WESTON. I'll try to explain how you got here. Do you remember what year it is?

JOHANNA. Of course, I know what year it is. I'm not stupid. This is 1884.

WESTON. It's 2097 now.

JOHANNA. Are you saying that I slept for over two hundred years?

WESTON. No, you were asleep for only a short period of time. My colleagues and I found a way to travel back in time. We also found a way to bring objects and people forward, but we have to be very careful.

JOHANNA. This is absolutely absurd.

WESTON. At first, it was inanimate objects, such as rocks, and then plants. We selected desolate areas, so as not to disturb the population. Then we began experimenting with mice and other small animals, sending them only a few hours back. Eventually, we were able to send them over one hundred years into the past and return them to our present. We had by this time . . .

JOHANNA. Kind sir, please excuse me. I really don't know what this is about, but I'm feeling much better, thank you, so I'll just be getting on my way.

WESTON. Where would you go?

JOHANNA. Why, I'm going back to Lexington Avenue and Twenty-third Street. That's where I live.

WESTON. The location you know as Lexington Avenue and Twenty-third Street no longer exists. You left all that behind you when we brought you forward.

JOHANNA. Well, why can't you send me back?

WESTON. By our calculations, after exhaustively poring over historical records, we learned that you died on this date as a result of being hit by a runaway feed wagon.

JOHANNA. But I didn't die! Look at me! I'm as alive as you!

WESTON. If we were to send you back, you would either die from that accident, or if we waited until after the wagon passed, it would change the course of history.

JOHANNA. I want to go home! I want to go home!

WESTON. I'm afraid you're going to be with us for awhile.

About the Editor

For twenty-seven years, Catherine Gaffigan has worked in theatre, television and film as director, producer, actress and teacher. As an actress, she made her New York debut opposite Dustin Hoffman in *Journey of the Fifth Horse*. She toured the country for two years in *Cabaret*, played Lady MacBeth, did stints in summer and winter stock, made many television commercials, suffered the agonies of soap opera life, and appeared in both Broadway versions of *Whose Life Is It, Anyway?* Her films include *Julia* and Brian DePalma's thriller *Sisters*. Since 1971, she has taught Master Classes in Acting in her own New York studio. In 1987, she produced and directed the North American premiere of *Lady Susan*, based on the Jane Austen novel, for the Jane Austen Society. She subsequently directed *Deals and Deceptions, Restaurant Romances, An Evening of Hilarity and Hidden Agendas, The J.A.R.* (world premiere), *Dance Me to the End of Love, Tom and Viv*, and *Murder in the Cathedral.* Catherine holds a BA in English from St. John's University and an MFA in Drama from The Catholic University of America in Washington, DC. She also trained in the New York studio of James Tuttle.

Ordering Information

To order additional copies of *By Actors, For Actors,* just send $7.95 per book (specify volume number) plus $2.50 postage/handling for the first book and $1.00 for each additional book (NYS residents, please add sales tax) to: Excalibur Publishing, 434 Avenue of the Americas, Suite 790, New York, New York 10011. Checks and money orders should be payable to Excalibur Publishing. For Master Card and Visa orders, please include type of card, your name as it appears on the card, card number, expiration date and your signature. For further information, call 212-777-1790.